THE
MADISON AVENUE

**FOR PEOPLE WHO CAN'T COOK AND DON'T WANT
OTHER PEOPLE TO KNOW IT**

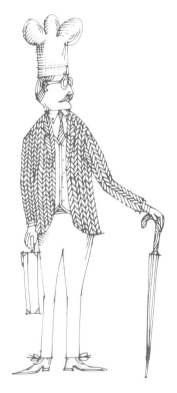

by ALAN KOEHLER
Illustrated by Murray Tinkelman

HOLT, RINEHART AND WINSTON
NEW YORK • CHICAGO • SAN FRANCISCO

"a loaf of bread
a jug of wine
and $65 thou"

...ANON.

PUBLISHED SIMULTANEOUSLY IN CANADA BY HOLT, RINEHART
AND WINSTON OF CANADA, LIMITED

LIBRARY OF CONGRESS CATALOG NUMBER: 62-17067

DESIGNER: BEN FEDER

85005-0112
PRINTED IN THE UNITED STATES OF AMERICA

Iɴ a large Madison Avenue advertising agency, with many diverse accounts, it is impossible for one man to know very much about all, or conceivably about any, of these accounts. And even a top-notch agency man gets just two or three good ideas a year, not enough to go round. Therefore a Madison Avenue adman must survive by ingenuity alone. He must appear to know a great deal about a great many subjects which he actually knows little or nothing about. And he must be skilled in adapting his few ideas to a wide variety of purposes. He must make a paucity seem a plethora. This is why he is customarily paid $65 thou a year.

THIS book is called The Madison Avenue Cook Book because it tells you how to appear to know a good deal about cooking when actually you know little or nothing. And how to make two or three basic ideas seem like an embarrassment of riches. In a decade of Madison Avenue cooking for friends and enemies, the author has avoided the slightest suspicion that he cannot cook. Nor is he by any means dismissed as a mere chip off the old Betty Crocker. Apparently it is only his future in communications which keeps him, in fact, from joining the kitchens of Grand Vefour or Laperouse.

On Madison Avenue you quickly learn that people who say nothing know nothing. If you seriously wish to conceal your helplessness in the kitchen you can't just keep quiet about it. You must, instead, tell everybody you can cook the pans off practically anybody... and must also, alas, produce "proof" to back up your boasts from time to time. Fortunately no artifice is so effective in concealing the fact that a person cannot cook as ... cooking! Yes, now you can keep the secret that you can't cook safe — *through cooking!* Little need even your most worldly or suspicious guest suspect that dinner isn't really dinner at all, but merely a ruse to conceal your inability to cook!

IMAGINE! All you need to use The Madison Avenue Cook Book with success are:

    (a) the utter inability to cook

    (b) the desire to conceal (a)

    (c) the following tools:

        1 pan
        1 pot
        1 frying pan
        1 lid
        1 knife
        1 fork
        1 spoon
        1 can opener
        1 coffee pot
        1 blender
        1 stove

There's nothing more to buy!

In arranging any ruse, the temptation is to go too far. Before we discuss what to do, let us mention what not to overdo. Serve cocktails as cocktails, not camouflage. Let the drinks flow freely, but not ad infinitum. Guests maddened by hunger don't care what they eat; those maddened by drink don't know. And tempting though it may be to serve your first few dinner attempts under cover of total darkness, don't. A single flickering candle in the middle of a table set for six may seem both prudent and intimate, but will defeat your purpose. For nobody can really taste food unless he's had a good look at it first.

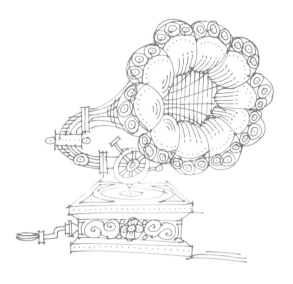

AND don't feel, as so many diffident cooks apparently do, that original-cast recordings of Broadway musicals, loudly played, provide the ideal accompaniment to (because they are such a distraction from) dinner. Let music play quietly on, but let vocal selections, if you must have them, be in a language not understood by the guests. Jazz makes food and wine nervous. The best idea are muted 18th and early 19th century string ensembles, even if everyone detests chamber music, because they stir up little eddies of elegance which trade up the dinner.

SUCCESSFUL Madison Avenue cooking depends upon an undeviating philosophy and point of view. Remember you are not perpetrating dinner but a deception. Your ravishing food notwithstanding, your primary concern is to mislead, however fortuitously you may nourish, your guests. Money, regretfully, cannot be an object. Only the choicest fresh meats and produce may be admitted to your kitchen. Your steaks and chops must be so thick that they can only be conspicuously consumed. The voluptuousness of your chickens derives from Rubens rather than Reuben's. Your lettuces are little lotus-eating lettuces. And, besides being drowsily drunk with their own nectar, your fruits are flagrantly out of season.

MONEY alone cannot buy the best of the best cuts of meat. Nor can they be identified by sight or feel, as the best produce can. Only your butcher knows for sure which they are, and you must have earned (besides money) his respect and devotion to get them. This is most easily and quickly done, even if you are a total stranger, by asking him to show you around his refrigerator. Even the iciest butcher's heart thaws as he ushers you into his sanctum sanctorum—his Grail room—and eulogizes his cooling apparatus, charcoal purifiers, air circulation, and elegant meats hanging with their exposed surfaces turning black, all of which you must feign to believe are a thick cut above other butchers'. This chilly five minutes is all you ever need per butcher; a butcher never forgets.

SUPERB produce requires neither so much money nor the devotion of the greengrocer to obtain. The best strawberry is easy to identify because it is staggering under its own juicy weight. And gentle breeding alone restrains the best tomato from bursting with ripeness in public. Yet most shoppers choose underripe specimens—resistant melons, obdurate avocados—instead of desirably deadripe ones. Deadripe produce will not keep, true, but who wants to keep it? Apparently everybody; greengrocers live literally up to their name and sell everything, naturally green or not, green. Some greengrocers even quarantine "overripe" produce and cut the price; this is what to buy, and the last possible moment before preparation of the meal begins is the time to buy it.

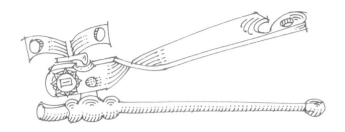

READY-PREPARED foods are used wherever possible. Their use, should anyone have the temerity to raise the question, must be deprecatingly denied. Of course their wrappers, jars or cans are thrown down the incinerator before the first guest arrives, and they are always doctored somehow so even their own Aunt Jemima wouldn't know them. (No dish may ever go to the table anyway without at least one Mystery Touch ingredient, identification of which you perennially postpone.) But let a certain honesty, that will later be interpreted as modesty, creep obliquely into your telephoned invitation to guests: "Come on over a week from Thursday for a drink about seven, and maybe I'll open a can of something so we don't have to go out." At dinner no one will dream that chances are this is exactly what you have done!

GARLIC—fresh or powdered—goes gaily into almost everything. Use as much as you can without losing the nerve to deny under cross-examination that you've used any at all. Even people who say they loathe or are allergic to garlic don't and aren't, provided you can convince them that it isn't there. Garlic, anonymous, is universally loved. In addition to garlic, herbs and spices provide the foundation of Madison Avenue cooking. Those necessary are few, and they are absurdly simple to use. Your hand must be lavish. Never worry about whether you're using too much, only too little. When in doubt (and when not), too much is always better. You may, if you wish, excuse yourself to your guests and appear to snip fresh unidentified herbs from a window box, and then go ahead and use dried ones.

STAPLE HERBS AND SPICES

basil
bay leaf (powdered)
bouquet garni
chives
curry powder
garlic powder
oregano
pepper (cracked)
rosemary
salt (plain and hickory smoked)
tarragon

WINE, of course, must be served, but only one wine is necessary through the meal. The Madison Avenue Cook Book cannot, in its integrity, endorse the prevalent practice of decanting inferior wines, and trusting to the elegance of the decanter to conceal the wretchedness of the wine. Because while it is true that most people cannot recognize a good vintage, it is also true that they instantly recognize a ghastly or domestic one. However, dryness is confused with superiority in the public mind. And so you'll make many more points with a routine bone-dry wine than with a superlative fruity one.

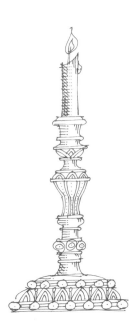

You're lucky if you have a cramped, contorted little kitchen with little if any working surface. If you have a large kitchen with a lot of working surface, eliminate much or all of it. Working surface has nothing to do with cooking. But the less of it you have, the more your cooking will be admired. If you will be observed at work in the kitchen, as you must surely arrange to be, take care that any lighting other than daylight is ''indirect'' and comes from a source well below eye level. The overhead lighting typical of most kitchens casts a clinical pall over everything, including the cook.

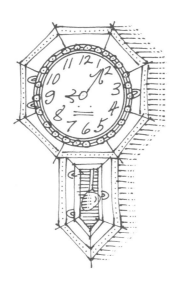

SOME delicacies, like our succulent vegetables and our hearty BBD&O, take time to prepare. So let them. For the Madison Avenue cook is a seeker only after status. He pursues the short-cake and eschews the short-cut. Anyone should choose for himself another image (and another text) if he wishes merely to commit hurry curry or equivalent. Some of our recipes also require you to spend much more time in the kitchen than with your guests before dinner. This may or may not seem a disadvantage. But you further dignify your cooking if you join your guests only in time (and perhaps only in order) to eat it.

THE quality of your crystal, china, silver and linen need not be 57th Street, provided that it seems to be. (Feature just one of your grandmother's own heirloom conversation pieces—obtainable at most thrift shops—in your service.) Searing hot plates contribute more to prestige than searing hot food. But don't be misled by those restaurateurs who feel that hot plates excuse food that's entirely cold. You may wish to omit a warning that plates are hot and let a guest more memorably make the point for all.

We have already observed that money can be no deterrent in Madison Avenue cooking. Yet, while it would cost more, one may not have help at dinner. Swear though you may that the girl came in only to serve, no one will believe she didn't do the cooking too, especially if she's Swedish, French or colored. Rejoice: serving dinner yourself gives you the chance to appear Effortless — popularly and erroneously assumed to be one of the hallmarks of people reputed to be great cooks!

HELPLESS though you are, never allow guests to assist in even the most irrelevant preparation for dinner. There must be the implication of something mystical in even the way you stir. The impression that something wonderful happens when *you* boil water vanishes instantly a guest boils any for you. After dinner, dissuade any guest from helping to clear the table. For your kitchen is busy building the image of a secret sacred little shrine where nothing gross, like garbage, or even merely banal, like washing dishes, can occur, and where used crystal, china, silver and linen are probably discarded.

A DETAIL vital to the success of your cuisine is to keep The Madison Avenue Cook Book concealed whenever guests are at large. (You may feel more confident if you have a number of authoritative prop cook books on prominent permanent display, like the stage-luggage law books in a lawyer's office, but these remain uncracked.) No one may know that your repertoire includes only those recipes here. Claim freely to be able to cook everything. And claim to cook it all from scratch; you soak your own beans, stir up your own mayonnaise, simmer your own stock. Probe others for their cooking secrets; within moments appear to grasp, consider and dismiss them; and laughingly refuse to divulge a one of your own—a job easier than it might be because of course you actually have none.

Do not confuse excellence with complexity. Do not be dismayed at the childlike simplicity of these recipes. The Madison Avenue Cook Book offers proof positive that the simplest dish can create the most awesome impression. Remember that your audience is easily fooled—even world-renowned cooks are more beholden to the ignorance of the eaters than to the excellence of the eaten. Try to think positively of not being able to cook as an *asset;* while there's a saying about cooks who spoil the broth, so far there's none about non-cooks who spoil it. But trial runs are recommended. Dress-rehearse even the simplest dishes here with servants or relatives before producing them for guests.

Warning! 🖙 **Never let yourself be lured out of your own kitchen and into another to cook. Things that you turn out hands down at home have a way of defying duplication by you abroad, and leaving you up a creek without a paddleford!**

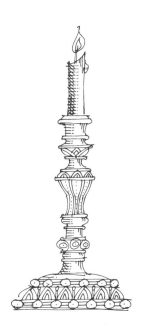

HERE, then, is our setting: Martinis have been encouraged to mellow, but not permitted to maul, our guests. Ethel Merman and Judy Garland have been retired, and a silken skein of Scarlatti spins from nowhere. Candles cast a confident warmth over the table. The crystal tinkles, the silver glints, the wine gurgles, and the aroma of haute cuisine (in reality none other than that of garlic) wafts in from the brave indirectly-lit little kitchen. Shall we now proceed to the pièce de resistance—that ingenuous handful of fool-proved recipes with which anyone can conceal forever the fact that he cannot cook by promoting the belief he *can*?

HORS DERVISH

Our first recipe is a felicitous one to begin the cooking part of the Madison Avenue Cook Book because it completely captures the spirit and calls for no cooking at all. Buy the blackest loaf of black bread you can find (bakeries of middle-European extraction are apt to bake the best) and slice it thin. Cut off crusts and cut slices in 2-inch squares. Open the costliest can of plump pink Portuguese sardines, chilled. Cut sardines in half amidships, and put half on each square of bread. Beside each sardine arrange one large and several small pieces of chutney imported from Bombay, chilled, with a little of the syrup. Curtail the supply or no one will be hungry for dinner.

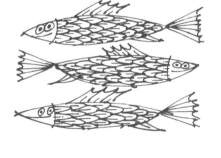

black bread
sardines
chutney

CHICKEN LOVERS SAUTE

Mercifully, saute is merely the French word for pan fry. Blend 4 tablespoons of flour and a teaspoon each of rosemary, oregano, cracked pepper, hickory smoked salt and garlic powder. Dredge a pound of freshest chicken livers (first cut apart lobes of large livers still joined together) in the mixture individually. Melt 2 tablespoons of butter in frying pan and add a clove of garlic sliced thin. Place a few livers in frying pan, and dust some of the remaining spiced flour over each. Saute slowly and after 4 or 5 minutes turn and dust the cooked sides (you eventually use up all the spiced flour as the rest of the livers are cooked). Livers are done when lightly browned, and must not be overcooked. Pass at once, with toothpicks and small napkins. Continue sauteing livers from time to time during the cocktail period, cooking only enough to go around at any one time.

1 lb. chicken livers	1 tsp. hickory smoked salt
4 tbsps. flour	1 tsp. garlic powder
1 tsp. rosemary	2 tbsps. butter
1 tsp. oregano	1 clove garlic
1 tsp. cracked pepper	serves 4-6

Soup "Exotic Flavor"

Cold soup is pedestrian enough served in summer, but in winter takes on gourmet overtones. The most important ingredient in this particular soup is garlic, from which the soup, of course, takes its name. Here is our first chance to use our blender. Mash 3 cloves of garlic, peel and chop an onion fine, and liquefy in the blender. Then liquefy 5 ripe tomatoes, peeled and chopped fine. Stir 3 tablespoons soy oil, 2 tablespoons tarragon wine vinegar, and a cup of beef stock (a bouillon cube dropped in hot water) into the liquefied vegetables. Add salt and pepper. Chill in refrigerator. Serve in plates or cups frosted in freezer. Pass separate dishes of chopped cucumber, tomatoes, green pepper, onion and cubes of stale white bread, if you feel like it, to be added to the soup at the table. Just before serving soup stir in a cup of icy vodka. Deny presence of the vodka, and, of course, the garlic, if necessary under oath.

3 cloves garlic	1 tsp. cracked pepper
1 large onion	1 cup vodka
5 large ripe tomatoes	optional:
4 sprigs parsley	chopped cucumber
3 tbsps. soy oil	chopped tomatoes
2 tbsps. tarragon wine vinegar	chopped green pepper
	chopped onion
1 cup beef stock	cubes of stale white bread
1½ tsps. salt	serves 4

28

Black Bean Summer Soup "McCann Can"

This soup would seem merely offbeat to serve in summer, because it is so hot and so heavy, were it not for a kind of Baked Alaska touch which elevates the dish to royal rank and establishes it as a hot-weather specialty. Open a can of condensed black bean soup, and stir slowly into it an equal measure of light cream, over the lowest possible flame. Add a teaspoon of curry powder, and a half teaspoon each of cracked pepper and salt, and a quarter teaspoon each of garlic powder and powdered bay leaf, and continue heating and stirring until the soup seems about to seethe. Add the juice of one lemon, from which you have reserved several paper-thin slices, and stir on until the soup returns to the seething point. Meanwhile, sour cream is chilling and thickening (but not freezing) in the freezer, and deep capacious cups, preferably delicate white Limoges to contrast with the color and heartiness of the soup, are heating in the oven. Pour seething soup into cups, add a blob of cold sour cream the size of a large matzo ball to each, pop a paper-thin slice of lemon on top, sprinkle more cracked pepper over all, and serve and eat instantly before temperatures equalize. Those who wish to stir or blend the sour cream into the soup miss the point; frown upon them.

1 can condensed black bean soup	½ tsp. salt
1 equal measure light cream	¼ tsp. garlic powder
1 tsp. curry powder	¼ tsp. powdered bay leaf
½ tsp. cracked pepper	1 lemon
	1 small container sour cream
	serves 2-3

SPECIALITE DE LA MAISON "KAY DALY*"

This scavenger soup is named for one of the great Madison Avenue cooks, who invented it from water and leftovers. She makes it so well she finds she need cook nothing else to maintain her wide reputation as a master chef, as well as to clear the decks in the refrigerator. She actually only more or less invented it because by its nature the soup is kind of reinvented every time, which makes the recipe imprecise. But you always proceed roughly the same way, whatever you do within reason turns out well, and this is how:

Fill your pot, which turns out to be a large one, 3 quarters full of cool water, add the whole chicken and chicken necks, bring to a bare boil and keep at a soft simmer for an hour. Add garlic cloves sliced almost through several times, plus bouillon cubes, vegetables, spices, leftovers, leavings, remains, and bones. Continue simmering for 2 to 4 hours. Turn off and leave overnight at any point if you get tired of it all, but then be sure to simmer it some more the next day. Strain whole thing through a dishtowel, and skim off fat. Cut chicken—and any other cooked meat—into tiny cubes and add to strained liquid. Reheat and serve. Or reheat, chill overnight (soup should jelly; if it doesn't, simmer a couple of hours longer, rechill) and serve.

water	1 tsp. powdered bay leaf
1 whole cleaned chicken	1 tsp. bouquet garni
1 lb. chicken necks	leftovers, any:
3 or 4 garlic cloves	limp celery tops
6 bouillon cubes	languid carrot tops
2 white radishes	indigent pea pods
6 small onions	sad scallion tops
6 carrots	discouraged cucumber ends
1 tomato, quartered	wilted watercress
½ lemon, rind and all	other demoralized vegetables
1 tbsp. salt	steak leavings
1 tsp. cracked pepper	roast remains
1 tsp. tarragon	bereft bones
1 tsp. basil	serves 6-8

*with or without whom this book would have been impossible

LEEK "TRANSIT GLORIA"

Here is our last chance to use our blender and our only one through which to appear conversant with the leek, the member of the onion family even more chic than the shallot : Mince white part of 3 leeks and an onion, all of average size. Saute them, stirring constantly, in a couple tablespoons of butter for several minutes. Meanwhile you have peeled and sliced or diced very fine 4 average size raw potatoes, which you now add to the leeks and onion along with 4 cups of chicken consomme. Cover and simmer for 20 minutes. Blend relentlessly in blender until surely smooth. Remove, add 2 cups light cream and 2 scant teaspoons each of salt, cracked pepper and dried chives. Heat slowly, stirring constantly, until ready to boil. Serve in heated cups or mugs, with a sprinkle of cracked pepper and chives on top of the soup. (Served cold, this soup turns into Vichysoisse, with all the s's sounded, but don't acknowledge it.)

3 medium leeks
1 medium onion
2 tbsps. butter
4 medium potatoes
4 cups chicken consomme

2 cups light cream
2 tsps. salt
2 tsps. cracked pepper
2 tsps. chives
<u>serves 6</u>

EGGS A LA RUSE

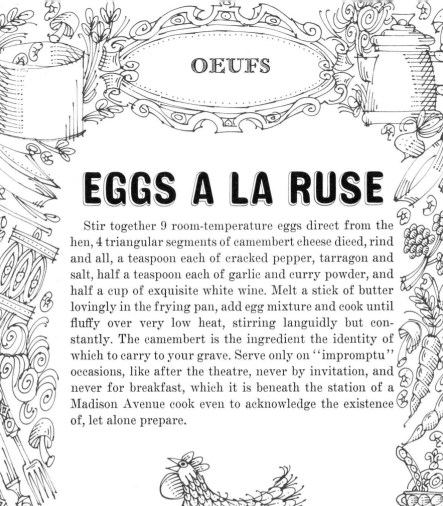

Stir together 9 room-temperature eggs direct from the hen, 4 triangular segments of camembert cheese diced, rind and all, a teaspoon each of cracked pepper, tarragon and salt, half a teaspoon each of garlic and curry powder, and half a cup of exquisite white wine. Melt a stick of butter lovingly in the frying pan, add egg mixture and cook until fluffy over very low heat, stirring languidly but constantly. The camembert is the ingredient the identity of which to carry to your grave. Serve only on "impromptu" occasions, like after the theatre, never by invitation, and never for breakfast, which it is beneath the station of a Madison Avenue cook even to acknowledge the existence of, let alone prepare.

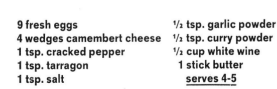

9 fresh eggs
4 wedges camembert cheese
1 tsp. cracked pepper
1 tsp. tarragon
1 tsp. salt

½ tsp. garlic powder
½ tsp. curry powder
½ cup white wine
1 stick butter
serves 4-5

Eggs Benedict "Arnold"

This is the recipe to choose if you will be observed by your guests at any time during your preparation of eggs, for here you get the chance to improvise a double boiler, which in itself casts the result in an occult light. As the bottom of your double boiler use whichever is larger, your pot or your pan, and as the top whichever is smaller. Bring water to a gentle boil in the bottom. Lower the top into the boiling water and melt a package of cream cheese and a tablespoon of butter in it. In the coffee pot, since it's the only available vessel, scald (but don't boil or it will curdle) a cup of light cream, and stir into cheese and butter. Add a half teaspoon each of salt and cracked pepper and a quarter teaspoon of garlic powder. Break 6 eggs gently into the sauce and let set briefly. But before the whites are firm stir eggs into the mixture, add the sherry, and continue stirring until all has thickened. Serve with chopped fresh chives or parsley on split and toasted English muffins. The revolutionary unpoachedness of the eggs and omission of the ham, together with the particular brand of English muffin endorsed, is what gives the dish its name. EGGS BENEDICT ''ARNOLD'' may legitimately be accompanied by a dozen little sauteed sausages.

1 pkg. cream cheese	6 eggs
1 tbsp. butter	2 tbsps. sherry
1 cup light cream	chives or parsley
½ tsp. salt	4 English muffins
½ tsp. cracked pepper	optional:
¼ tsp. garlic powder	12 little sausages
	serves 4

33

OEUFS

Omelet "Avenue Madison"

No one can claim to cook unless he can talk knowledgeably about cooking an omelet. The Madison Avenue cook alludes from time to time to his ethereal omelets that the sleepiest stirring of southern breeze would surely waft away. But while the omelet recipe and procedure is simplicity itself, the successful execution is, in the author's experience, impossible. Therefore this is a recipe to memorize, and never ever for a Madison Avenue cook (for whom the initial cooking failure is the ultimate disaster) to attempt to actually prepare:

The omelet requires its own pan which is used for no other purpose, and which is wiped carefully clean and never washed with soap. (Since we are never going to make an omelet we may omit this pan.) Cook each person's omelet separately. Stir into 2 just-laid eggs a generous tablespoon of milk and half a teaspoon of salt. Melt 2 tablespoons of butter in the omelet pan. Get it hot but don't let it brown. Then pour in the eggs and begin loosening the edges immediately as they set with a spatula (which you also need not own). Lift edges to allow uncooked mixture on top to run underneath. When the omelet is still soft and creamy on top but otherwise cooked, lift one edge with the spatula and roll it over onto itself as you slide it from pan to plate. (If you wish to not-make an omelet a still more difficult way, shake the pan back and forth constantly with one hand while you stir the eggs in a circular motion constantly with the other, categorically impossible to do, as the omelet cooks.)

34

POISSON

SOLE OF DECEPTION "FTC"

We include this recipe because without it we would have no fish dish at all. And because the stature of a cook is instantly jacked up a notch when a guest comes upon a whole cooked grape in anything. For each guest borrow a presentable oven-proof dish, with sides, from a friend. Place a filet or two of fresh but not necessarily pedigreed white fish, which you bill as Dover sole flown from England the night before, into each, on top of a tablespoon of butter. Spread a mixture of half sour cream and half mayonnaise, into which you have blended a little lemon juice and a lot of sliced mushroom caps (see CHAMPIGNONS) sauteed with a lot of seedless white grapes, liberally over fish. Bake for 20 minutes at 350. Never on Friday.

½ lb. white fish filet
1 tbsp. butter
¼ cup sour cream
¼ cup mayonnaise

juice of ¼ lemon
2 or 3 mushroom caps
2 dozen white grapes
serves 1

WESTPORC "CONNECTICUT"

Por(c)(k) is a delicious but inelegant meat unless something is done to it, and what in this case you have done to it no one may ever guess. Buy a loin roast of pork allowing a pound per person. Rub roast with salt, cracked pepper and rosemary, and put it, fat side up, on the broiling pan (& rack) from the broiler of your stove. Roast it uncovered in the oven at 350 degrees, allowing 40 minutes a pound. Remove roast from oven and let stand (it will continue to cook) while you prepare a FAIRFIELD SAUCE from 1 part horseradish, 2 parts applesauce and 3 parts sour cream stirred together with a little salt and pepper. Carve meat in kitchen and spread gently heated sauce liberally over thick slices. Or allow meat to heat sauce before serving.

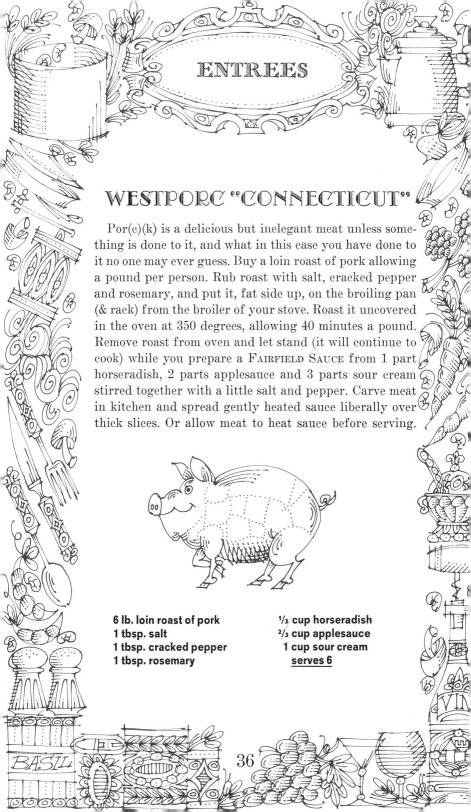

6 lb. loin roast of pork	**⅓ cup horseradish**
1 tbsp. salt	**⅔ cup applesauce**
1 tbsp. cracked pepper	**1 cup sour cream**
1 tbsp. rosemary	**<u>serves 6</u>**

Roastettes "Rosser"

People who wouldn't eat a lamb kidney if they knew what it was will if they don't. Have the butcher, perhaps against his will, remove the bone and much of the fat from one 3-inch thick loin chop of baby spring lamb per person, roll chop around half a lamb kidney cut lengthwise, wrap it around with bacon, and tie it with a string. Arrange roastettes with one of the lamb sides up on the broiling pan and sprinkle lavishly with garlic powder, rosemary, oregano, hickory smoked salt and cracked pepper. Broil 10 minutes in preheated broiler. Turn, apply spices to uncooked sides, broil 10 minutes more, and serve.

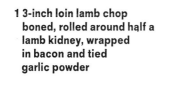

1 3-inch loin lamb chop
boned, rolled around half a
lamb kidney, wrapped
in bacon and tied
garlic powder

rosemary
oregano
hickory smoked salt
cracked pepper
<u>**serves 1**</u>

Shell Steak in the Bag "Ogilvy"

Successful cooks do as little to food as possible to achieve whatever desired results. They know that flame is more foe than friend to food and that most cooks ruin their cooking cooking. All vegetables, and meats except for pork and chicken, benefit from ''undercooking,'' and absolutely nothing benefits from overcooking. To serve lamb or beef other than rare, except in stew, is to commit a crime against nature, like putting sugar on tomatoes. Inquire of your guests whether they prefer their steak rare, medium or well done, but serve it only rare.

☞ Know thy oven. Know thy broiler and burners too. Every stove has a metabolism all its own which can be determined only by experiment. Timings given throughout The Madison Avenue Cook Book are for the average stove, and in life there's no such thing.

Rub a 3-inch shell steak thoroughly with soy oil. Press into the 2 sides of the steak a total of: 2 cloves of finely chopped garlic, 1 teaspoon each powdered bay leaf, bouquet garni, cracked pepper and hickory smoked salt, and finally half a cup of course bread crumbs. Put steak into a brown paper bag and roast 35 minutes at 375 for acceptably rare. Bring steak to table in the now burned & blackened bag, publicly remove and carve. The implication that roasting in the brown paper bag contributes crucially to the taste of the meat is in no way minimized by the fact that it doesn't.

1 3-inch shell steak	1 tsp. cracked pepper
2 tbsps. soy oil	1 tsp. hickory smoked salt
2 cloves garlic	½ cup coarse bread crumbs
1 tsp. powdered bay leaf	1 brown paper bag
1 tsp. bouquet garni	<u>serves 2</u>

Steak "Schpeppervescence"

Two things that an American (as opposed to a French) cook usually won't do are: pan fry, rather than broil, a steak, and cover it with enough pepper to make STEAK "SCHPEPPERVESCENCE." Buy a regal sirloin or porterhouse an inch and a half thick or more. Allow ¾ of a pound per person. On a table, spread cracked pepper over an area roughly the size of the steak. Press the steak onto the cracked pepper, then lift it up and put it down again several times, until steak is covered with all the pepper it will hold. Turn steak and press pepper firmly into meat with the heel of your hand. Apply pepper the same way to the other side. Cut a little fat from the meat and use it to grease your frying pan which must be blazing hot; sear the steak on one side for a minute, then lower flame and cook more gently for 4 or 5 minutes. Turn. Sear and cook as before. Remove steak from pan, and pan from fire. Pour an ounce of cognac per serving of meat into the pan. Stir into the juices in the pan, and pour over the steak.

**1½-inch thick sirloin
or porterhouse
cracked pepper
cognac
each ½ to ¾ lb. serves 1**

LIVER "UPPER"

No tricks here, but the very thought of a 2-inch thick slab of calf's liver is too much for most people, so they must never know this is what you started with. Rub the liver steak with soy oil and put it on the broiling pan. Cover liberally with garlic powder, oregano, rosemary, hickory smoked salt and cracked pepper to form a thick crust. Broil 5 minutes in preheated broiler, turn, apply spices to other side and broil 5 minutes more. Liver should be very spicy and crusty on outside, very pink in the middle, and served sliced thin, smothered with onions you began preparing an hour and a half before. All you did was put 3 or 4 tablespoons of soy oil in your frying pan, peel a couple of giant Bermuda onions and slice them into the pan, cover tightly with your lid and let steam slowly over low heat with just an occasional glance to see if anything is sticking and to add a spoonful more of soy oil if so. For the last 10 minutes, during the time the liver is broiling, salt onions and cook uncovered to brown them.

2-inch thick slab of
  calf's liver, at least
    ½ lb. per person
soy oil
garlic powder
oregano

rosemary
hickory smoked salt
cracked pepper
1 large Bermuda onion per person
salt
each ½ lb. <u>serves 1</u>

ENTREES

POULET "OLE"

Slice a clove of garlic and brown it in 4 tablespoons of soy oil in the frying pan. Rub salt and pepper generously into a 2-pound chicken cut up for frying, and brown the chicken in the oil. Then add ½ teaspoon each of powdered bay leaf, tarragon and basil, plus ½ cup of good white wine and cook slowly, covered, for 40 minutes. After which, if people are late or you don't feel like eating yet, you can continue cooking practically forever if you just add a little extra wine from time to time.

1 fat clove garlic
4 tbsps. soy oil
  salt
  pepper
1 2-lb. chicken, cut up

½ tsp. powdered bay leaf
½ tsp. basil
½ tsp. tarragon
½ cup white wine
<u>serves 2-3</u>

Breasts of Chicken "Honey Chyle Style"

Buy a large breast of freshly killed and immaculately cleaned chicken for each person and have it split. Rub soy oil into each half by hand. Arrange on broiling pan bone side up. Put several dots of butter on high points of chicken so when it melts it will run down over rest of breast. Scatter dried tarragon, hickory smoked salt, and cracked pepper prodigally over all and broil for 8 minutes, spooning some of the juices from the bottom of the pan over the chicken after 4 minutes. Turn chicken, apply butter, tarragon, salt and pepper as before, and broil for another 8 minutes, basting again after the first 4. Turn chicken, baste, spread honey over chicken, broil 5 minutes more. Yet again turn chicken, baste, spread honey, and broil for 5 final minutes. Keep the honey part of the recipe under wraps to conceal your feet of Claiborne.

1 breast of chicken per person, split
soy oil
butter

tarragon
hickory smoked salt
cracked pepper
orange or apple blossom honey
each breast <u>serves 1</u>

ENTREES

KASEROLE "KASELOW"

Peel and slice an eggplant in ½-inch slices. Sprinkle slices with salt and let stand 1 hour. Chop onion and saute till transparent in a little soy oil. Add lamb, salt, pepper, garlic, and rosemary, and saute till meat is browned slightly. Remove everything from frying pan, add remainder of the soy oil, dip eggplant slices in flour, and brown on both sides. Borrow a 3-quart casserole, partly because you don't have one and partly because casseroles taste better in somebody else's casserole. Arrange alternate layers of eggplant and meat, and top with the sliced tomatoes. Bake 1 hour at 350. Blend yogurt, egg yokes, flour and mix well. Pour over casserole. Bake 15 minutes longer, or until brown.

2½-lb. eggplant
1 small onion, chopped
3 tbsps. soy oil
2 lbs. ground lean lamb
2 tsps. salt
1 tsp. cracked pepper

½ tsp. garlic powder
½ tsp. rosemary
3 or 4 tomatoes, sliced
1 small container yogurt
4 egg yokes
½ cup flour

serves 6-8

Hot Market Tip

Prevail upon your great & good friend the butcher to cut 6 or 7 inches off the very tip of a beef tenderloin he has recently received. Have him pound a piece of beef fat thin, roll up the tenderloin in it, and tie it round several times with string. Broil it, lying down, for 8 or 10 minutes, loaded with as much garlic powder, powdered bay leaf, bouquet garni, hickory smoked salt and cracked pepper as will stay on the rounded surface of the fat without falling off. Turn, load on the spices (most of which run off in the broiling anyway), and broil 8 or 10 minutes again. Who will guess exactly what ambrosial cut of meat this, all rolled up, is?

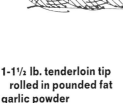

1-1½ lb. tenderloin tip
   rolled in pounded fat
garlic powder
powdered bay leaf

bouquet garni
hickory smoked salt
cracked pepper
serves 2

Baked Beans "Durstine & Osborn"

No one knows why already cooked canned baked beans don't turn to mush when you cook them some more, but they don't. Empty the pork and beans into your pot. Add the wine, brown sugar, honey, powdered bay leaf and cracked pepper, stir, and simmer gently for several hours until the beans have cooked down to their original consistency. Beans can be cooked almost indefinitely as long as wine is added whenever the mixture has cooked down, and the longer they cook and the more wine you add the better and more "home made" the flavor becomes. Even Bostonians will beg you for this undoubtedly "authentic" and "original" recipe, but never divulge more than your name, rank and serial number.

5 16-oz. cans pork and beans
2 cups wine dry as alum
1 cup dark brown sugar
1 cup orange or apple blossom honey
1 tbsp. powdered bay leaf
1 tbsp. cracked pepper
<u>serves 10-12</u>

STATUS STEW

Unlike a statesman, a Madison Avenue cook can't wait till he becomes elder to perfect his beef stew. Because of its powerful reverse-snobbism gear, any stew cooked by any cook in an upper income bracket is likely to have status. But STATUS STEW is statusier than others because the only liquid used to cook it in is vintage Beaujolais instead of stock, a detail we never fail to neglect to mention to guests.

Put the butter into your pot and brown the beef and the two large onions, sliced, in it. Slice and add the garlic. Mix in the flour. Brown the bacon separately in your frying pan, and add it, together with the bouquet garni and salt and pepper. Pour enough wine over the meat to cover. Simmer for 2 hours. Skim off the fat. Add the (peeled) baby onions and cook for 15 minutes more. Add the raw sliced mushrooms and cook for 15 minutes more. Sprinkle with chopped parsley and serve.

2 lbs. elegant rump steak cut in 1½ inch cubes	2 tsps. bouquet garni
½ stick butter	2 tsps. salt
2 large onions	2 tsps. cracked pepper
3 cloves garlic	excellent (red) Beaujolais
1 tbsp. flour	2 dozen tiny onions
½ cup diced lean bacon	1 cup mushroom caps, sliced
	2 tbsps. chopped parsley

serves 4

46

LEGUMES

LEGUMES
"UNAMERICAN"

The Madison Avenue cook's vegetables—including corn-off-the-cob, asparagus, carrots, peas, spinach, broccoli, green beans, etc.—are unforgettably superb simply because he uses no water to cook them. He first selects only the most succulent raw material at the greengrocer's, fussing over the bins until he's sure he has the best (though he has been known to use frozen). He gently peels, scrapes, shells, snaps, washes, removes from the freezing compartment, or whatever, the vegetable. He puts a couple of generous spoonfuls of butter in his frying pan (which, to be explicit, is a heavy one, preferably enameled, and better yet one made in France by Le Creuset) and puts the vegetable—it can still be frozen solid—in too. He never fails to add a mystery touch—e.g. honey and dark brown sugar for carrots or dried onion flakes for peas or slivered almonds for green beans or an unidentified spice for anything—as well as salt and cracked pepper. He puts his tight-fitting lid on the pan and gently steams the vegetable over low heat for perhaps an hour, or until barely done, taking an occasional peek to be sure all is well. It always is. The Madison Avenue cook would rather run himself down the Disposall than mix two vegetables together.

    12-16 oz. vegetable, fresh or frozen
    2 tbsp. butter
    1 mystery touch ingredient
    1 tsp. salt
    1 tsp. cracked pepper
    serves 3-4

47

Handy "Mystery Touch" Chart*

LEGUME	MYSTERY DASH
ASPARAGUS	rosemary
BROCCOLI	rosemary
CARROTS	rosemary
CORN	rosemary
GREEN BEANS	rosemary
PEAS	rosemary
SPINACH	rosemary

*see Appendix A

48

POMMES DE TERRE

Something for the Boise

Since a baked potato gives you the maximum potato credit you can get anyway, the Madison Avenue cook troubles himself to do nothing to potatoes but bake them. He chooses only firmest Idaho beauties with schoolgirl complexions. He scrubs each potato with a brush under running water, and rubs it well with soy oil. Each potato is baked in foil gathered loosely around it, with a hole for the potato to look out of, for an hour in a 375 oven, or till tender through and through to a fork. If served with butter, potatoes should be drowning in it; remove a scoop of potato to make room, and let the butter melt well into potato, with salt and pepper, before bringing to the table.

Idaho potatoes
1 tsp. soy oil each
½ stick butter each
salt
pepper

Sweet Potatoes "What Reallyam"

There is no tuber more maligned than the sweet potato: most cooks rebuff the unadulterated sweet potato and have to have it canned or candied or bandied or marshmallowed or gussied or fussied in some demoralizing way. Many people think they don't like sweet potatoes because they don't even know what an honest-to-God plain sweet potato tastes like. Thus our touche mysterieuse for the sweet potato: we do nothing to it at all but bake and butter and salt and pepper it like a white potato—and wait for everybody to tell us that they've never tasted anything quite like it in their life, and what on earth did we *do?*

sweet potatoes or yams
1 tsp. soy oil each
½ stick butter each
salt
pepper

50

Currier & Chives

Any potato thrives on CURRIER & CHIVES. Into a half pint of sour cream stir half a teaspoon each of curry powder, chives, salt, brown sugar, confectioners' sugar and cracked pepper, and a quarter teaspoon garlic powder. Taste, and add more of any of the ingredients that may seem desirable. Remove large scoop of potato, white or sweet and hot from the oven, being careful not to puncture or rip skin at sides or bottom so nothing can run out, and place beside potato. This is to make room for the butter and the CURRIER & CHIVES. Sprinkle salt copiously into cavity and on adjacent scoop. Put generous hunk of butter into cavity and smaller hunk on removed potato. Apply sauce munificently. Top with more pepper and chives.

½ pint sour cream
½ tsp. curry powder
½ tsp. chives
½ tsp. salt
½ tsp. brown sugar
½ tsp. confectioners' sugar
½ tsp. cracked pepper
¼ tsp. garlic powder
serves 4

51

Champ(ignon)s Elysees

As a Madison Avenue cooking status symbol, mushrooms sit with the cooked grape, the slivered almond and the omelet-to-talk about. They are child's play to prepare. Fresh firm mushrooms only, please. There's nothing wrong with the stems, but since they're imperceptibly tougher than the caps the Madison Avenue cook discards them. He then sautes the whole caps ever so gently in a little butter into which, perhaps, he has slipped a slice of garlic clove, and serves them as hors d'oeuvres. Or he sautes them sliced thin and serves them over meat, or as a separate "vegetable," or why not folded into Eggs a la Ruse? Add mushrooms to any dish, except those few with which they are obviously incompatible, like coconut cake, and you improve it. But, except in stew, always cook them first. They take a very few minutes, and you can tell just by looking at them when they are done.

mushoom caps
butter
1 slice garlic clove

Salad
"Caesar & Desist"

The only ingredients that need ever find their way into our salads are the tenderest innermost leaves of Boston or bibb lettuce, and lush tomato slices or sections, peeled. (Iceberg lettuce is perhaps the most aptly named plant in the world, and should be avoided as though you were the Titanic with another chance.) And the only dressing we require is the peerless "BONNES SAISONS." This exquisitely simple salad, exquisitely simply dressed, never palls or pales, and you will become as famous for it alone as you'd be if you knew a hundred salads, because try as he might no one (except a Madison Avenue confrere) thinks he can quite duplicate it. The civilized world prefers salad served after, tolerates it served during, and summarily rejects it served before the entree, and you'll have to too or you can't be a Madison Avenue cook.

Boston or bibb lettuce
tomatoes
salad dressing "BONNES SAISONS"

53

SALADE

SALAD DRESSING "BONNES SAISONS"

Here we rely upon the packaged salad dressing mix labeled "garlic" (and, if we wish, upon the accompanying calibrated cruet which the packaging folk also make available). So far so ordinary, you may think. But now we add to the prepared mix ¼ cup of tarragon wine vinegar, 2 tablespoons of superb red wine, a clove of garlic mashed (the garlic clove takes up residence in the dressing bottle indefinitely) and, most important, ⅔ cup of soy oil, bought in any health food shop. The secret is really in the soy oil, and once you have tasted it—or more accurately not tasted it—soy is the only oil you'll ever use unless you're Popeye. We have, as you remember, no salad bowl, so our lettuce and tomatoes will have to be hand-dipped in dressing. Hand-dipping is, of course, merely a make-do procedure, yet we cherish it, for if you can contrive to be observed in the act of hand-dipping you add a redoubtable je ne sais quoi to the completed salad.

1 package "garlic" prepared
   salad dressing mix
¼ cup tarragon wine vinegar
2 tbsps. red wine
1 garlic clove, mashed
⅔ cup soy oil

54

BUFFET FREUD

Steak "Nature in the Raw is seldom Mild"

We mention only two of the status-improving virtues of this elegant raw ground steak experience: Many people won't eat it, but in not doing so are embarrassed at their own gaucherie, which accrues to the chic of the chef. And, while the dish requires no cooking, and next to no preparation, it nevertheless helps paint your culinary lily: for though anyone can see no one cooked it, he also believes only a consummate cook would serve it.

Simply mix the ingredients below together thoroughly, and serve, shaped into a neat ellipsoid, with a sprinkling of capers, on a couch of tender lettuce. If you, like so many Madison Avenue agency people, are a gifted actor or actress, you may wish to mix each guest's portion individually, and with some flourish, at the table.

(If you are worried about too many of your guests going hungry because they can't or won't eat raw meat, you may wish to turn the other chic by offering them a choice, cold buffetwise, of this dish or the one on the next page.)

½ lb. ground raw
    blue-blooded steak
1 fresh raw egg
1 tsp. salt
1 tsp. cracked pepper
½ tsp. garlic powder
½ tsp. thyme
1 tsp. caper juice

1 tsp. Worcestershire sauce
½ tsp. Tabasco sauce
1 tsp. soy sauce
1 tbsp. chopped parsley
2 tbsps. minced onion
capers
bibb or Boston lettuce
serves 1

Jellied Pigs Feete "Cone & Belding"

While the way to a man's hearse lies inevitably through his stomach anyway, a dish like PIG'S FEETE "CONE & BELDING" might seem calculated to speed him unduly on his way. Yet the Madison Avenue cook includes this receipt, as Granny would say, in his repertoire for these reasons: (1) Anything other than jelly that's jellied contributes crucially to prestige. (2) There is an undeniable élan in constructing a dish from lowly organs, linings, glands, nodes, ganglia and extremities. (3) Because, being jellied, it must be prepared in advance, you can probably prevail upon the chef of a nearby French restaurant to prepare it for you and still take all the credit.

Wash 6 pig's feet, and wrap them in cheesecloth to keep their girlish figures. Simmer them in water to cover for 3 hours, adding boiling water as necessary. Then add a large sliced onion, a sliced lemon, a teaspoon each of powdered bay leaves and cracked pepper, 2 cloves of garlic sliced nearly through several times, and half a dozen or so borrowed (because our cuisine has no other use for them) whole cloves. Simmer another hour. Strain the stock through a dishtowel. Add a little excellent white wine, the drier the better, and a teaspoon of salt. Add a chopped pimento if you care for color. Remove skin and bones and put feete and stock in refrigerator until firmly jellied. This triumph is ideal as part of a buffet which offers other things to eat too. Delicious though it is, it remains one of those rare dishes that enhances one's reputation as a cook rather less when eaten than when not; with luck no one will touch it, though either way you're way ahead.

6 pig's feete	2 cloves garlic
water	6 whole cloves
1 large sliced onion	1/8 cup white wine
1 sliced lemon	1 tsp. salt
1 tsp. powdered bay leaf	1 chopped pimento
1 tsp. cracked pepper	serves 6

BASIL

Stuffed Softsell Crab

Stuffing almost anything with almost anything else seems to have a salutary effect upon the stuffed, upon the stuffee, and upon the estate as a cook of the stuffer. This particular stuffed creation requires no cooking besides. Buy one deadripe avocado per person and a couple extra in case any have already departed this life, which you can't tell till you open them. For each person buy a quarter pound of flaked fresh (as violently opposed to canned) crabmeat, just caught. Arrange 2 chilled avocado halves, seed removed to be sure, on a bed of bibb lettuce, inner leaves only, on each plate, along with quartered hard cooked eggs and fat flagrantly bloodripe tomatoes, cut into eighths. Heap crabmeat high in well of each avocado half. Serve with a large bowl of ANONYMOUS SAUCE and flowings of champagne to drink. This recipe should be called stuffed avocado instead of stuffed crab, but it's not.

1 avocado per serving	1 hard cooked egg each
¼ pound flaked fresh crab each	1 tomato each
bibb lettuce	ANONYMOUS SAUCE

57

Anonymous Sauce

No problem here. Simply stir some of the most expensive prepared mayonnaise from the best gourmet shop within reach together with an equal quantity of SALAD DRESSING "BONNES SAISONS," some capers, some of the caper juice, a squirt of lemon, a fling of cracked pepper, and serve. Warning!: remember, you did it all yourself!

prepared mayonnaise
equal quantity salad dressing
  "BONNES SAISONS"
capers
caper juice
lemon
pepper

ENTREMETS

Fresh Fruit "Way Out of Season"

Build anything more elaborate than a better mousse for dessert and the world will not necessarily beat a return path to your door. Dessert should close the meal gently, and not in a pyrotechnic blaze of glory. No cultivated feeder, already well fed, thanks his host for confronting him with a dessert so elaborate that not to eat it is simply rude—like refusing to watch one's host blow up Bloomingdale's. Impressive though a DOUBLE SOUFFLE OF CROWBARS "ALLENE TALMEY" or flaming EUGENIA SHEPPARD'S "PIE," or equivalent, may be, do not prepare them. Instead:

Obtain at whatever cost glowingly ripe fresh fruit as far out of season as possible. Serve the fruit au naturel, with a little eau de vie poured discreetly over it. A subtle touch is to use a liqueur which has the same flavor as the fruit and then, of course, to deny the addition of the liqueur. You will soon acquire the reputation for serving the most exquisitely flavored fruits known to man. (When serving strawberries, cut a triangular cone which includes the stem from the top of each berry, pour liqueur into the hollow inside, and arrange the berries so that they stand top side up until each berry closes itself over the liqueur, as it soon will.) Though almost all combinations of fruits and spirits are interchangeable, likely ones are:

pears & cedratine
peaches & champagne
marrons & Kahlua
raspberries & framboise
oranges & Grand Marnier
blueberries & gin

pineapple & Pernod
blackberries & blackberry brandy
strawberries & Chartreuse
pitted cherries & kirsch
sliced grapes & brandy
plums & mirabelle

Fruits, unlike vegetables, may be mixed together with impunity, but fruits can only be fruits, never salad.

59

WALTER LOWENGRINS

Now it's entirely too folksy to serve your own cookies in your own house at any time. Particularly after dinner when they tend to do to the rest of the food what chintz would to a formal salon, or the presence of a Greenbay Packer to your guest list. Yet these cookies—actually a cross between the praline, the muffin, and the cookie—can get the mileage, reputationwise, of a Madison Avenue bus when they are baked exclusively for hospitalized friends (whose prognosis is favorable).

Mix thoroughly: 4 heaping cups old-fashioned whole grained oatmeal and 2 cups brown sugar (1 dark, 1 light) and 2 sticks of butter melted but not browned and a scant teaspoon salt and 2 overflowing tablespoons of real vanilla. We have been very good about sticking to our original table of equipment; it has been too perfect to last: we need muffin tins. Fill muffin cups a little more than half full of mixture and do not tamp it down. Place in 350 oven and bake 15 minutes, or until mixture sizzles and rises to the tops of the cups. Allow LOWENGRINS to cool in cups for 15 minutes before removing.

4 heaping cups old-fashioned whole grained oatmeal	2 sticks butter
1 cup dark brown sugar	1 scant tsp. salt
1 cup light brown sugar	2 tbsps. real vanilla extract
	makes 24 LOWENGRINS

CAFE-ER CAFE

The secret of serving coffee that seems to be freshly ground and brewed yet can't be, because we have no grinder and just a coffee pot with no innards, is to use instant espresso, in the same quantity as you would regular instant coffee. Put a rounded teaspoon per cup into the coffee pot, add vigorously boiling water, add brandy with abandon, add a dozen or so bittersweet chocolate nuggets per pot, stir, and pour coffee at the table. The more beat up the coffee pot the more your coffee will be admired. A Madison Avenue cook would sooner turn into a dripolator than serve coffee during the meal. Keep quiet about that chocolate.

water
instant espresso

brandy
bittersweet chocolate nuggets

CREAM AND SUGAR

Cream and sugar, served with coffee at the end of a meal, are like a dish of celery, olives and radishes at the beginning and bread and butter in the middle—both a bore to fool with and a distinctly deleterious anti-gourmet touch. Cream, sugar, celery, olives, radishes, bread and butter should be omitted. Diehards who insist on sugar or cream or both may be put off if you reveal the presence of the brandy in the coffee. (Which, of course, is no reason for you not to be also serving brandy separately in your polished snifters, as you surely are.)

no cream
no sugar

61

APPENDIX A

Variation Handy "Mystery Touch" Chart

ASPARAGUS	basil
BROCCOLI	basil
CARROTS	basil
CORN	basil
GREEN BEANS	basil
PEAS	basil
SPINACH	basil

An Appropriate Musical Programme

CHICKEN LOVERS SAUTE
Mozart, K.384, suite, "Abduction from the Seraglio"

SPECIALITE DE LA MAISON "KAY DALY"
Handel, "Water Music"

SOLE OF DECEPTION "FTC"
Schubert, Op.114, D.667, Piano Quintet in A, "The Trout"

SALAD "CAESAR & DESIST" WITH DRESSING "BONNES SAISONS"
Vivaldi, Op.8, Nos.1-4, Concerti for Violin and Orchestra, "The Four Seasons"

.FRESH FRUIT "WAY OUT OF SEASON"
Repeat of Concerto "Winter" above

CAFE-ER CAFE
Beethoven, Op.113, "Ruins of Athens"

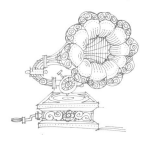

63